On

Martin Sherman was born i[...]
in London since 1980. His plays include: *Passing By*,
Cracks, *Rio Grande*, *Bent*, *Messiah*, *When She Danced*, *A
Madhouse in Goa*, *Some Sunny Day* and *Rose*. Adaptations
include: *Absolutely! (Perhaps)* (Pirandello), *The Cherry
Orchard* (Chekhov) and *A Passage to India* (from E. M.
Forster). Musical: *The Boy from Oz*. His screenplays
include: *The Clothes in the Wardrobe* (US title: *The Summer
House*), *Alive and Kicking*, *Bent*, *Callas Forever*, *The Roman
Spring of Mrs Stone* and *Mrs Henderson Presents*. His plays
have been produced in over fifty countries and he has
received nominations for two Oliviers, two Tonys and two
Baftas.

Martin Sherman

Onassis

based on material from Nemesis *by Peter Evans*

Published by Methuen Drama 2010

1 3 5 7 9 10 8 6 4 2

Methuen Drama
A & C Black Publishers Limited
36 Soho Square
London W1D 3QY
www.methuendrama.com

Copyright © 2010 M. G. Sherman Ltd

Adapted from *Aristo* by Martin Sherman, originally
published by Methuen Drama in 2008

Martin Sherman has asserted his rights under the Copyright, Designs and
Patents Act 1988 to be identified as the author of this work.

Based on material from *Nemesis* by Peter Evans

ISBN 978 1 408 13999 8

A CIP catalogue record for this book is available from the British Library

Typeset by Mark Heslington Limited, Scarborough, North Yorkshire
Printed and bound in Great Britain by Good News Digital Books, Ongar

Caution

For the Denissi

Mimi
Maria
Sofia
and Maritina

Onassis

Onassis is a revised version of the play which, under its former title *Aristo*, opened at the Chichester Festival Theatre in 2008. *Onassis* was first performed at the Derby Playhouse on 14 September 2010 and opened at the Novello Theatre on 12 October presented by Aukin/Vogel for DAP Ltd, Playful Productions, Act Productions and Bob Bartner in association with Jamie Hendry and David Lightbody. A Chichester Festival Theatre Production in Association with Derby Live.

Costa	Gawn Grainger
Dimitra	Sue Kelvin
Eleni	Liz Crowther
Theo	Robert Hastie
Onassis	Robert Lindsay
Jacqueline	Lydia Leonard
Yanni	John Hodgkinson
Maria	Anna Francolini
Alexandro	Tom Austen
Musicians	Ben Grove
	Graeme Taylor
Ensemble	Rachael Barrington
	Suanne Braun
	Nigel Carrington
	Matthew Romain

Director	Nancy Meckler
Set and Costume Designer	Katrina Lindsay
Lighting Designer	Ben Ormerod
Composer	Ilona Sekacz
Sound Designer	Andrea J Cox
Video and Projection Designer	Lorna Heavey
Choreographer	Lizzi Gee
Casting Director	Gabrielle Dawes CDG

Characters

Costa
Dimitra
Eleni
Theo
Onassis
Jacqueline
Yanni
Maria
Alexandro
Musicians
Ensemble

Act One

Two **Musicians** *enter and sit on stage. They play bouzoukis. Three* **Men** (**Costa**, **Yanni** *and* **Theo**) *and two* **Women** (**Dimitra** *and* **Eleni**) *enter and mingle amongst the musicians. Some are singing. Some stop, and the others pick up the song. They are all (except for* **Theo**) *over sixty and tastefully dressed. They are the* **Chorus**. *When they are alone together they inhabit a dream-like space.*

Chorus
    Sto pepromeno sou na dinis simasia
    Ken a prosechis pos vadizis sti zoi
    Otan kimase alos grafi istoria
    Ke kapios pezi ti diki sou dip sichi

Yanni *opens a bottle of wine and pours glasses for the others.* **Eleni** *is pasing around pastry.*

Costa (*referring to the music*)   This was his favourite song . . .

Dimitra   I remember.

Eleni (*handing pastry to* **Theo**)   I baked these. Here, it's good for you, you don't eat enough . . .

Theo (*laughs*)   You're treating me like a grandson . . .

Eleni   I wish I had a grandson . . .

They each sit in a chair and, together, they conclude the song.

Chorus
    Olie chou me grameno
    Pou to lene pepromeno
    Kekannas na sve borina tapo fiyi
    Den I parchi theoria
    Outre trena oute plia
    Kio kathenas to palevi opas kseri

Costa *rises and addresses the audience.*

Costa   What can I possibly tell you? In antiquity there were gods. They shared all of mankind's virtues and faults and embodied all human concepts and emotions. But the gods went to extremes; they had an unnatural attraction to the cream of man and woman kind, who they were prone to ravage. And so demigods were born, and later still, those who the mythologists called heroes, who were not necessarily heroic, not in our terms, but behaved with the sweep and grandeur of the gods and yet remained humanly vulnerable. Movie stars and politicians come to mind. And, let's face it, it is difficult not to walk in their shadows. I, for one, certainly do. I am the second in command to Aristotle Onassis. Aristo. Ari. I share his secrets and execute his commands. I touch the sun, so to speak, and of course I sustain burns, but really, I'd rather do so than walk placidly on earth, day after boring day. I suppose I become more than I am, and yet also somewhat less than me.

Pause.

Now, you are about to witness Aristotle Onassis ... that's two Ss in the centre – one of the world's richest men, a notorious ship-owner and much else – and my boss – my, in the classical sense, hero – in an early encounter with Jacqueline Kennedy, wife of the 35th president of the United States. It is 1963, by the way. Jacqueline has recently lost a baby, who died three days after his premature birth. Her sister, Lee Radziwell, the wife of an impoverished Polish prince but also, as it happens, the current mistress of Aristotle Onassis, has urged Onassis to invite Jacqueline for a restorative cruise on his yacht. When she is sure other guests will be present Jacqueline accepts the invitation, despite her husband's disapproval, and allows her sister to bring her onto the yacht and into the hands of fate.

Aristo *appears, standing alone, looking out to sea. He is Greek, in his sixties, dressed in a dinner jacket. He sings a melancholy melody, quietly, to himself.*

Aristo
> Tha giriso lipimeni panagia
> Eche gia
> Min les to marazi
> Mathe filakto na min kremas
> Na les den piraziu
> Tha'rthi aspri mera ke gia mas . . .

Jackie *steps out of the shadows. She is in her thirties. She is American, elegantly dressed.*

Jackie   Please – don't stop.

Aristo   I didn't realise you were there.

Jackie   Didn't you?

Aristo   An interesting question. I may be lying.

Jackie   Oh.

Pause.

Do you often lie?

Aristo   Only when I have to. So, yes, I often lie. But, as you may notice, I always tell the truth about lying.

Jackie   That's refreshing. Most of the people I know really can't tell the difference.

Aristo   Ah. Politicians.

Jackie   I'm afraid so.

Aristo   The God of Lies has a soft spot for politics.

Jackie *(laughs)*   Did the Greeks really have a special god for dishonesty?

Aristo   My dear, we had a god for everything. Everything human. It would have been Hermes, as he was also the god of theft. And commerce. They seemed to think the two belong together.

Jackie   Don't they?

Aristo   Of course. In my world, nothing quite adds up as nature intended. Two and two do not necessarily make four, not if four goes against my interests.

Jackie   Do you really admit so easily to being a scoundrel?

Aristo   Yes. Thrilling, isn't it?

Jackie   Well, I don't know ...

Laughs.

Actually, yes.

Aristo   I make deals. The best deals never stand up to moral scrutiny. Every businessman and politician in the world knows that. I'm a pirate. Not unlike your husband.

Jackie   He would never admit to that.

Aristo   Then I *am* unlike him.

Jackie   Possibly. Possibly not.

Pause.

I like pirates. When I was a little girl I was bored to tears with Peter Pan and positively detested Wendy, but I had a huge crush on Captain Hook. I still do, I suppose. He was a bit of a rascal, wasn't he? – dangerous and in danger at the same time – I mean, that ticking clock .... He had edge. Of course the problem with Captain Hook was his lack of elegance. And he had that really horrid, tatty ship ...

Aristo   Not a yacht.

Jackie   No. Not a yacht.

Aristo   So your dream man is Captain Hook on a yacht.

Jackie   Umm. Preferably with both hands intact.

Aristo   Ah. As I suspected. You have a carnal soul.

Jackie   I am going to tactfully change the subject. Tell me about the song you were singing.

Aristo It concerns an insatiable woman. She must make love ten times a night.

Jackie You don't approve of changing a subject.

Aristo Not unless I do it.

Jackie Then the trick is to make you think you've done it.

Aristo No. I can't be flattered.

Jackie I wouldn't dream of trying.

Aristo Actually the song was about love.

Jackie Love?

Aristo Yes. You know, it's rumoured to be a human emotion. Highly overrated in my opinion. Do you know rebetiko?

Jackie I don't think so. Unless it's a wine.

Aristo It's what we call our songs – some of them – the melancholy ones mostly – the ones about misfortunes of fate – the ones played by a bouzouki, which is actually an instrument from antiquity, a favourite of the gods supposedly. This particular song at one point says I have cried salty tears when I am away from you. *Salty*. It's an old favourite and I am very fond of it although I detest all of its sentiments. After all, the only free people – really free – are those who love nothing or no one. Don't you think?

Jackie I think you're pretending not to be sentimental.

Aristo In other words, I'm lying. Well, it's as I said. Second nature. Although I am not sentimental. I must warn you about that. Do not imbue me with American qualities. I'm from a much older race. You go back to the Mayflower; we go back to Mount Olympus.

Jackie Well, then, you were not lying.

Aristo Don't be silly. Of course I was. Do you see those lights on the shore?

Jackie   I believe *you* have just changed the subject.

Aristo   I have. Look at the lights, please. It's Izmir. Where I was born. It was called Smyrna then.

Jackie   Wasn't Homer born there?

Aristo   He was. As well.

Jackie   Then Smyrna was twice blessed.

Aristo   Precisely. I'll show it to you tomorrow. I'll show you my father's warehouse, if you like; it's still there. He was a tobacco merchant. Did well for a Greek living in Asia Minor. I'll show you where Fahria's was. The local whorehouse. Do I shock you?

Jackie   I think you're trying to. Actually, my father was known to visit whorehouses. I find that not unacceptable.

Aristo   I was very popular at Madame Fahria's when I was a teenager. Because I carried vast supplies of my father's finest tobaccos with me.

Jackie   Is that where you learned about commerce?

Aristo   Of course. And even there I got the better deal. Madame Fahria's would have suited you.

Jackie   Careful.

Aristo   That was a compliment. I'll show you the port tomorrow, which is where I first saw the Fourth Turkish Cavalry the night they rode into Izmir, then Smyrna, intent on driving out the Greek population. They were dressed completely in black and carried their scimitars unsheathed and drawn. Have you ever seen a scimitar? It would be unusual if you had; in Washington the weapons are mostly unseen, isn't that true? No matter, I'll show you one, I have a scimitar locked away on the boat. I have no idea why. I should hang it in a stateroom, but it might seem vulgar. I realise perfectly that you might consider other sections of this yacht vulgar, in concert with most of the fashionable people who snicker at this uppity Greek behind his back.

They focus on my barstools – the ones made of whale's scrotums. But if I had simply pretended it was some kind of leather they would have admired them. Why pretend? Don't you agree?

Jackie   That was a breathtaking subject-change.

Aristo   Not necessarily. The subject remains carnal. I'm about to tell you how I was fucked by a Turkish soldier.

Jackie   Bravo. I didn't see that coming. Were you really? Tell me. In detail. Please.

Aristo   Oh, I intend to. I was sixteen, it was 1919, and the Turks arrested my father and sent him to prison. Our house was commandeered by a young lieutenant who was rather extraordinary, possessing both taste and curiosity, qualities wasted killing people. I liked him. He took to me. We became lovers. Which allowed me to sneak food and money to my father in prison, but I cannot – or will not – pretend my capitulation was based solely on that. I enjoyed it. You see, he inserted his cock into rather surprising and delicate parts of my body, and I could feel its rhythm, its music, its sometimes senseless lurching, at other times its sublime control, and pleasure and pain were indistinguishable from one another – are you enjoying this, by the way?

Jackie   Well, it's not Homer.

Aristo   Good. Then you are. The point, my dear, is – whilst being fucked, I had a revelation. This, I thought, must be, to some degree at least, what a woman feels with a man inside of her. I had discovered a great secret, a secret that would make me an extraordinary lover. I knew from that moment on the sensations a woman has when she is being made love to. And so it only follows that I know how to prolong that pleasure. When I screw a woman, I am in it for the long haul, so to speak. I inhabit the house. Some men just drop in for a visit. Isn't that true? That question is purely rhetorical.

Jackie   Perhaps that entire story is as well. Perhaps it's the biggest lie of all.

Aristo   Perhaps. Do consult your sister. I will confess a very recent lie to you. The one you suspected. I knew you were there, listening. I know every footstep on my boat, feel every shadow. I never have to turn around to know what's behind me. Or ahead of me, for that matter. The past, the future, all connect when I'm here. Here on my ship. Captain Hook with all my hands on deck.

Jackie (*stares at him for a second, then – softly*)   Tick-tock ... tick-tock ...

Aristo   As crocodiles go, you're very attractive.

Smiles.

Tomorrow I'll show you the street I grew up on. I'll show you the bed in the house on the street where Aristotle Socrates Onassis grew into a man. I was, as you know, named for not one, but two philosophers. Tomorrow I'll show you whatever you need to see so you can understand me. And desire me. I'll show you an old life, and I promise you, my dear Mrs Kennedy – or may I now, after this illuminating conversation, address you as Jacqueline – or perhaps even Jackie – a new life as well. I am delighted you accepted my invitation to join us on this cruise. I shall see you in the morning.

The lights fade on the ship. **Aristo** *walks to the* **Chorus**, *smiles at* **Costa** *with immense satisfaction.* **Costa** *speaks to the audience.*

Costa   Well. A holiday flirtation.

Aristo *leaves.*

Costa (*to audience*)   But this is a world in which nothing is simple. There is a chequered history between Onassis and the Kennedy clan. There had long been bad blood between Aristo and Jacqueline's brother-in-law. That's Robert Kennedy. Brother to the 35th president of the United States. Attorney-general and heir apparent. Bobby. Now – Bobby Kennedy and Aristotle Onassis met for the first time at a cocktail party given by the English socialite Pamela

Churchill at the Plaza Hotel in New York City. Bobby
Kennedy and Onassis took an instant, visceral dislike to one
another. This was in the spring of 1953, the year Jacqueline
Lee Bouvier, as she then was, married John F. Kennedy.
The aforementioned Pamela Churchill was ... well, what
can I call her?

Looks to the **Others** *for help.*

Dimitra (*happy to oblige*)   A courtesan?

Theo   That word is no longer in use. Now they call it a
shrewd networker.

Dimitra   Umm ...

Costa   Yes. Thank you, Theo. Pamela was the former wife
of Randolph Churchill, the alcoholic son of the former
British prime minister, Winston Churchill, who was himself
a frequent guest on the yacht of ...

Holds out his hand.

Dimitra (*to audience*)   Aristotle Onassis.

Costa (*to audience*)   She, Pamela, had known Bobby since
1938 when his father Joseph P. Kennedy was the American
ambassador to England. She was a friend of Bobby's sister,
Kathleen Kennedy, and indeed at the age of eighteen, whilst
a weekend guest at the Kennedy home, had been raped by
Kathleen's father when he slipped into her bed late one
night.

Eleni (*disgusted*)   Ohh ...

Costa   That's the aforementioned Joseph P., who years
before, had been the lover of the movie star Gloria
Swanson, who had later and coincidentally had an affair
with Aristotle Onassis, who in the early 1940s was just
beginning to climb from the ruins of Smyrna to the world
of maritime tycoons, and was sleeping with other movie
stars as well, such as Veronica Lake and Paulette Goddard,
who later married the German novelist Erich Maria

Remarque, who had been a lover of Marlene Dietrich, who had, on separate occasions, slept with both John F. Kennedy, and his father Joseph P., the raping ambassador. Got it? Aristotle's infatuation with movie stars ended when he paid court to ...

Motions to **Theo**.

Theo   Tina Livanos.

Costa   ... the younger daughter of the greatest Greek ship-owning family, who he eventually married. Tina's older sister ...

Motions to **Yanni**.

Yanni   Eugenia Livanos.

Costa   ... would marry Aristo's chief business rival ...

Motions to **Eleni**.

Eleni   Stavros Niarchos.

Costa   ... who was, incidentally, a former lover of ...

Motions to **Dimitra**.

Dimitra   Pamela Churchill.

Costa   As indeed was Ari. I would call Niarchos Onassis' nemesis, but that word is better applied to Bobby Kennedy. Like Onassis, Bobby had a penchant for movie stars, although not to the degree of his brother John F., the 35th President of the United States, and indeed both brothers had famously bedded Marilyn Monroe, who you will be relieved to know, never met Aristo. Although he did offer her his yacht after she was fired by her movie studio, 20th Century Fox, which was run by Spyros Skouros, a fellow Greek, who happened to own a fleet of container ships, which Onassis had invested ten million dollars in; ships that would cut union costs by sixty per cent, thus earning the enmity of the labour racketeer Jimmy Hoffa, who was an associate of the Mafia boss, Sam Giancana, whose mistress was Judith Campbell, who was also sleeping with John F. Kennedy, whose brother Robert was an implacable enemy of Jimmy Hoffa, and had written a book about their conflict, the film rights of which were held by Spyros Skouros, who was, needless to say, a former lover of Marilyn Monroe.

All of the above-mentioned names suddenly appear on a screen behind their heads, lines connecting and criss-crossing one to another, as they had been mentioned.

I'm exhausted. If you find this a little heady, I can assure you – it is. But the secrets of powerful men, the men who rule the world, who are the real, if sometimes covert, centres of power, read astonishingly like a cheap gossip column. Well, actually not. Gossip columns are comparatively tame. Real life is far more complicated. Where were we?

Yanni *walks up to him.*

Yanni   We're up to Jiddah.

Costa   Oh yes. May I introduce Yanni ...

Yanni   Yes, please. Financial advisor to Aristotle Onassis. Perhaps it would be easier if I explained this part.

Costa   Only if you get straight to the point.

Yanni   Of course. Now, question mark? Why did Aristotle Onassis hate Robert Kennedy? Now, seriously speaking, I would say, if you allow me – Aristotle Onassis hated Robert Kennedy because of the Jiddah Agreement. Period. Full stop. That's my opinion.

Costa   Just give the basic facts ...

Yanni   Yes. Yes. If I may. Aristotle Onassis was working on, if I may be allowed to say so, an extraordinary deal with the Saudi Arabians that would have given him the rights to ship the bulk of the oil flowing out of the Arabian kingdom. I have to confess this would have made him as powerful as any nation state. Exclamation point! The Jiddah Agreement meant that Saudi Arabia and Aristotle Onassis would, between them, control the means of oil production and distribution, thus empowering the Arab nation to do without America. This deal, I would like to say, was signed by the Saudi foreign minister and waited only royal approval ... Dot, dot, dot ...

Costa   Fine. Thank you.

Yanni *sits.*

Costa   Now – let us recap. The Livanos sisters – Tina and Eugenia, remember? Tina married to Onassis, Eugenia married to Stavros Niarchos. Tina, needless to say, was sleeping with her sister's husband. She informed him about Aristo's impending – and top secret – deal with the Saudis. Niarchos was Onassis' most implacable rival. He was determined to stop the deal and knew that only the Americans could do so. Niarchos was, among many other things, a valued CIA informant, and he passed the information on to them. Finally, under pressure from the Americans, the Saudis backed down and the Jiddah Agreement was cancelled. The CIA was eager to hide Niarchos's involvement – they protected their informants. They were already aware that Onassis disliked Kennedy. So they planted clues that implied it was Robert Kennedy who had destroyed the Jiddah Agreement and Onassis bought it. Aristo was, of course, devastated and never forgave Bobby. Never!

Dimitra   Excuse me! There is someone you forgot!

Costa   Yes? Who?

A great orchestral opera theme is heard. The lights suddenly blaze and glow. The **Chorus** *look on in awe as* **Maria Callas** *sweeps in.*

Maria *motions toward the screen with a flick of her hand and the name* **Callas** *appears in huge letters, obliterating the other names.*

Maria *seems almost ready to sing; instead she looks at the screen, and then looks away in disgust.*

Maria The rest are pygmies!

Maria *walks away, furious.* **Dimitra** *goes to* **Costa**.

Dimitra Aren't you ashamed, you foolish little man? There are no gods anymore, but there was a goddess. And he destroyed her. What kind of hero is our dear Mr Onassis then? What kind of hero?

Maria Dimitra.

Dimitra Yes, Madame Callas.

Maria Tell me the truth – are there unmade beds?

Dimitra Unmade beds?

Maria Yes, you're the ship's housekeeper so I'm asking a very sensible question. Are there unmade beds? Or put it this way – does anyone else sleep in his room?

Dimitra No, Madame Callas.

Maria Ah. No. He sleeps alone.

Dimitra (*to audience*) I lied.

Maria (*to audience*) I would think she lied.

Costa (*to audience*) Of course she lied. Aristotle Onassis and Jacqueline Kennedy consummated their flirtation on the Ionian Sea, where the bright currents of the Aegean flow into Homer's 'wine-dark' waters. It was not only Jacqueline's sister who was displaced in his affections but also his real leading lady, the world's most revered opera star, Maria Callas. Her relationship with Aristo was the primary cause of his divorce from

Maria (*with contempt*) Tina!

Aristo *enters and sits in a chair, next to a bar. He is going through business papers. Occasionally, he looks out at the sea. He is in a different reality than the others.*

Costa Madame Callas wasn't like the rest of Aristo's women. Like him she had known the severities of war, like him she had overcome great difficulties to achieve riches and extraordinary fame. They fell in love with each other's past.

Dimitra   And then he destroyed her.

Maria   That's nonsense.

Costa   He destroyed your voice.

Maria   Stop it! Don't say that. You must not hate him for something he did not do. I destroyed my voice. I sit in my apartment every night and listen to my recordings. But when I am with him, on his island, on the boat, there is no need to listen to *myself*. Don't you understand? I feel the wind across my face. I look at the sea, look at the sky. How can I feel special when I stare at infinity? What's a *voice*? It's not a sound nature intended. Does someone shouting bravo substitute for the sea? How dare they give us the name 'star' when the real thing sits in an unknowable universe? My nights on his ship taught me humility. Everything I'm saying is rubbish. He wanted me as a woman. No one ever had before. It's as simple as that. No, it's not simple. He's a brute. Maybe I need that. No, that's not true. I can't explain it. What I do know is, it is not difficult being swept off one's feet. Living with the consequences is the hard part. So for years I did not sing, or sang intermittently, which is fatal. And now my voice is gone. Gone. I destroyed it, not Aristo.

Dimitra   Forgive me, Madame Callas, but you know how he felt about opera. Didn't he used to say that it always sounded like a bunch of Italian chefs screaming risotto recipes at each other?

Maria (*laughs*)   Yes.

Dimitra   Then it's inescapable, he's ruined you.

Maria   Ruined! What a word!

Costa   He is about to throw you over for the one woman in the world more famous than you.

Maria (*moves away*)   Who, may I remind you, is married. To the most powerful man in the world. No, not even Aristo can compare with that. He will do no such thing.

She enters **Aristo**'s *space. He looks up.*

Maria   The newspapers say . . .

Aristo   Newspapers lie.

Maria   I know newspapers lie. I know that better than anyone.

Aristo   Then don't talk about them.

Maria   I'm not.

Aristo   Good.

Maria   Nonetheless . . .

Aristo   What?

Maria   They say you were attentive . . .

Aristo   Attentive?

Maria   To Mrs Kennedy.

Aristo   Attentive is a stupid word. Servants are attentive. Courtiers are attentive. Are you accusing me of being a courtier?

Maria   When you want to be you *can* be. Oh, but I couldn't care less. Be attentive if you like. It doesn't matter at all to me.

Aristo   Then – please – don't bring it up.

Maria   Then – please – don't be photographed smiling at her.

Aristo   Don't you dare tell me who to smile at. Bitch.

Maria   Bastard!

Aristo   Putana.

Slaps her.

Maria   Malaka!

Slaps him back.

Aristo   Whore!

They stare at each other, then start to laugh and fall into each other's arms.

Maria (*looks triumphantly at the* **Chorus**)   What can I say – we're Greek!

Returns to the **Chorus**'s *space.*

In this country everything's a drama, everyone shouts. It's a way of life. And it means nothing. Of course he will sleep with other women, he's a Greek man, so what? I am a Greek woman – I know he will come back to me. I am his. That's all. Nothing else. His.

Gunshots.

Gunshots again.

Maria *leaves.*

Dimitra   Listen.

Yanni   Dare I say the most famous gunshots in the world? I'm serious.

Costa (*to audience*)   So. John F. Kennedy, the 35th president of the United States, is assassinated by ... no, *that* you know. But what you probably don't know – what even I, Aristo's closest confidant, still find – well, astonishing – is that Onassis flew to Washington the next day and stayed at the White House – was a guest at *The White House* – until the funeral. Invited by Lee Radziwell, at the request of her sister Jacqueline.

Aristo *is sitting at his desk. He opens a bottle of wine.* **Costa** *enters the room.* **Aristo** *looks up.*

Aristo   Have a glass.

Pours two glasses of wine.

Costa   Thank you.

Aristo   From our vineyards.

Costa   Yes, I can see.

Pause.

So?

Aristo   So?

Costa   What happened?

Aristo   You *know* what happened. It was on television, it's in every paper, you've seen it all.

Brushes newspapers on his desk aside.

Not a single newspaper says I was there. Funny how they always miss the big story. Actually, there was no story. I paid my respects. That's all.

Drinks.

Excellent wine. I was sober the entire time. That was quite an accomplishment. Stillness. Sometimes you achieve victory through stillness. But it isn't easy.

Costa   Aristo, tell me what happened.

Aristo   Nothing happened. You're such an old gossip. Nothing happened. It was a funeral. *But* you would have been proud of me. I didn't drink. And I didn't let them get me.

Costa   Get you?

Aristo   Indeed. Oh, now you're curious. Aren't you?

Pours himself another drink.

His brother. His brother. Well, well. They were all drunk. In the family dining room the night before the funeral. Bobby and his friends. They were singing Irish songs. It was what they call a wake, which is a very strange name, since it implies consciousness. The women were upstairs. Bobby apologised to me. For the noise. He didn't want to offend my European sensibilities. I explained that we also sing when we are sad. I even gave him a bit of a song.

Sings.

Ilie fonia pos afises na gini to kako
Skotosane to *stavraeto*
Ke ton avgerino

Pause.

I told him it was about a man who has fallen before his time. 'They killed the golden eagle, The morning star ...' He made a face, said it was too pretty. Not his taste. 'Neither are you, Mr Onassis. For Christ's sake, *my brother is dead!*' he shouted. 'What are you doing in our house? (*Pours another glass for* **Costa**.) Have another.

Costa   *And* ...

Aristo   And? And nothing. I was very calm. But he was beside himself. He said that he had been attempting through purely legal means, of course, to keep me from ever entering the United States again. And now I was there in the United States, in the White House, at his brother's funeral. Now, my friend, you must understand, he does not revere irony. He dislikes it; it's a Greek export. He kept offering me drinks and I kept refusing. I was determined to stay sober. I knew that would annoy him. I said the White House suggested dignity and I wouldn't presume to get drunk there. 'You won't let me get under your skin?' he said. 'No, no,' I said. 'I won't.' And I didn't I didn't. So. That's what happened. Nothing.

Costa   I don't believe you. You're much too satisfied with yourself.

Aristo   Well, why not? I returned with a present.

Takes a linen napkin out of his pocket.

Bobby. It's a teenage name, isn't it? Someone with bad skin who takes you to the high school dance. Bobby. Well, he began to tell the others about my money. He said I owned Monaco, which isn't strictly true. He said I owned my own airline, which *is* true. He said I owned much too much. Suggested I give it away. And then he grabs this napkin from the table and takes out a pen and proceeds to write on it. He was amusing his drunken Irish friends the night before they buried his brother. 'Aristotle Onassis,' he writes. 'Aristotle *Socrates* Onassis', I said; well, 'I, Aristotle Socrates Onassis, hereby give fifty per cent of my fortune to ...' and then he was stuck for a minute ... so he has a little mini-Kennedy-conference with himself, trying to decide where to take this joke, and then he has an inspiration! 'I, Aristotle Socrates Onassis, hereby give fifty per cent of my fortune to the poor of ... *Latin America* ...

Pours himself another drink.

They were drinking hard whiskey, of course. Not wine. And do you know why he chose Latin America. It turns out that fucker knows everything about me. How I got my start in Buenos Aires, for example. 'Some cigarette scheme,' he said, 'introducing Turkish tobacco to Argentina. Made your first bundle.' Oh yes, he expressed things very eloquently. Bundle! Well, there's truth in the word. I could see him studying my face – he wanted to see if I was shocked that he knew so much. And then – and he said this would impress me – he also knew that I was fucking an opera singer then – an *earlier* opera singer – and he pretended to fish for her name. 'Muzio, was that it, Claudine?' No, 'Claudia', I said. Claudia, 'Well, close enough,' he said. Yes. Close enough. I *was* impressed.

He polishes off the wine.

Aristo   Our island grapes are unappreciated. Of course, every Greek island makes its own wine. Ours is better, don't you think?

Costa *hands him another bottle.*

Costa   And the point . . .

Aristo   Ah! The point! The point was, the FBI had files
that detailed every moment of my life, every deal I'd ever
made, every woman I'd ever fucked – and Bobby Boy had
read them! On the beach, I imagine, like some summer
novel, cheap but unputdownable. And then, of course, he
couldn't resist a sanctimonious little lecture: 'You know, I
wouldn't care, finally, finally, I wouldn't care,' he said, 'if
somewhere in those voluminous files there was one kind
deed, one act of humanity, some gesture to someone less
fortunate than yourself. Grabbing is alright – we all grab –
but you have to give as well, that's the essence of a workable
society, isn't it? – grab *and* give? It's the basis of democracy,
which, yes, don't tell me, is a Greek word. I've memorised
your files. Claudia Muzio, see? *Memorised!* I know exactly
who you are.' 'Then you are more fortunate than I,' I said.

Looks at the napkin.

'I, Aristotle Socrates Onassis, hereby give fifty per cent of
my considerable fortune' – I added considerable – 'to the
poor of Latin America.' 'In perpetuity' – I added that as
well; might as well give it some style. I dated it and signed it,
and he held it up, but no one laughed. The joke had lost its
. . . fizz. Perhaps they remembered why they were there. He
just stared at me. 'I can't get your goat,' he said. 'No,' I said,
quietly – *calmly* – 'You can't.' 'My brother is dead,' he said
'You may not realise it – or care – but the future of this
country is dead as well. *Why are you here?*'

Pause.

Well, I didn't answer, did I?

Pause.

And that was my night at the White House.

Pause.

Stillness, you see. It works.

Rises, tears the linen napkin into small strips and throws them aside.

The skinny, shit-faced, puke-smelling, ass-eating little runt! Get my goat! Goat is a Greek delicacy. We eat them *and* fuck them!

Walks over to the **Chorus**.

And I'll fuck him and eat him too and spit him out and little pieces of him will scatter over the earth and land on outdoor barbecues in Minnesota and Dubrovnik and Thessaloniki and be consumed as little specs of ash on second rate, under cooked souvlaki! Get my goat! My 'goat' has just begun!

He grabs another bottle of wine and drinks it down almost in one gulp. He snaps his fingers to the **Musicians**, *who begin a song. He sings.*

Aristo and **Chorus** (*sing*)
  Imaste alania thya leta pethya mesastin piatsa
  Ke then tin tromazoun
  Ifortunes tin thiki masratsa
  Ke then tin tromaszoun
  I fortunes tin thiki masratsa
  Ti ta thes ti ta thes panda etsini zoi I
  Tha ye las ti tha kles vra thi ke proi

Aristo *starts to dance. The others applaud in time. Some of the others start to dance with him. Finally, the song finishes.* **Yanni** *hands* **Aristo** *another bottle of wine.*

Aristo *drinks, then goes to* **Theo**.

Aristo   So. My son? Tell me the truth. How is he doing?

Theo   Wonderfully, Mr Onassis.

Aristo   The truth. Don't butter me up.

Theo   Olympic Aviation Charter Business is now a profitable operation. Surely you know that.

Aristo   Of course I know that. I just wanted to hear you say it. It gives me ... fatherly pride. Pleasure. He's a good boy, isn't he?

Theo   He is, Mr Onassis. Everyone at the office loves him.

Aristo (*quietly*)   Everyone loves him?

Theo   You can be very proud of him. He's considerate, courteous . . . he's an extraordinarily nice young man.

Aristo   *Nice!!!!* There has never been a *nice* Onassis! Where is the bastard? I'll tear him limb from limb. Not to mention considerate and courteous! Hasn't he learned anything from me?

Theo (*amused*)   Well, actually . . .

Aristo   It's not a fucking joke. You have no idea how *dangerous* it is to be nice in my world. I am afraid for him. Do you understand? It's that woman, isn't it? That bitch. She's pasteurised him. She's made him safe to drink. I'll break her legs. I'll scar her face. I promise you! I will not have a nice son!

Aristo *storms off.*

Theo (*to audience*)   When you work for Mr Onassis you invariably say the wrong thing. But he gets over it. The storm arrives from nowhere. But then it leaves. And you're still standing. Yamas.

Costa (*to audience*)   Now. Aristo has two children by his wife Tina – Alexandro and Christina. Alexandro is . . . nice . . . and Christina difficult. Alexandro is in love with the former Fiona Campbell-Walter, subsequently the former Baroness Thyssen-Bornemisza, sixteen years his senior. Aristo worries about his children and he detests Fiona Campbell-Walter Thyssen-Bornemisza, perhaps, it has been suggested because she prefers not the father, but the son.

Aristo's *house.* **Aristo** *and* **Alexandro**.

Aristo   Your mother says she's a call-girl. That this Fiona of yours was paid 100,000 dollars to spend one night with King Farouk in St. Moritz.

Alexandro   But he's obese. That's too low a price.

Aristo   Then she's a stupid call-girl.

Alexandro   Not even you believe this one, papa.

Aristo   Don't use that fucking word. It's so sentimental. I'm bored with you. Go away. Do you ever hit her?

Alexandro   Of course not.

Aristo   Are you faithful?

Alexandro   Yes.

Aristo   I despair, I despair. Where's the *passion?* If you fight, if you strike her, if you walk away, it means there is some kind of feeling, and feeling is what's important, feeling means you are alive, unlike politeness, which is antiseptic, which is a desert, and then, of course, you *come back*, and you cry, and you say I am sorry, my love, and you buy her a diamond. Then you are a man.

Alexandro   I'm leaving.

Aristo   Not until I say you can go.

Alexandro   You told me to go away.

Aristo   I didn't mean it.

Alexandro   What *do* you mean?

Aristo   Very little. Get out. She's a spy.

Alexandro (*starts to leave*)   Goodnight.

Aristo   Don't you dare walk out on me. Your mother told me that Niarchos is paying Fiona to spy on us.

Alexandro   She's sleeping with Niarchos.

Aristo   Fiona?

Alexandro   Mother.

Aristo   That's beside the point. Your girl is a spy.

Alexandro   She doesn't need to be. Niarchos ... Uncle Stavro has bugged all our houses. And you've bugged all of his. Actually, you've bugged all of *our* houses as well. Silly for you to ask me questions when you've already heard the answers on tape.

Aristo   Look at you, standing there, looking bewildered, as always ...

Grabs **Alexandro** *and hugs him.*

You're a goddamned baby. Useless.

Pause.

You're a good boy.

Kisses him.

Your mother wouldn't lie.

Alexandro   She always lies. Just like you. Did you actually ever love her?

Aristo   There were moments. Life has moments. And there's a kind of satisfaction. And then the moment passes. And you want more. It will pass for you too. One day you wake up and look at her sleeping next to you and have nothing but contempt.

Alexandro   For her or yourself?

Aristo   Does it matter? It's still contempt.

Alexandro   What happened to the passion you were talking about?

Aristo   You still have the passion. But for someone else. How did you come out of my belly so green? If this Fiona is a spy I'll find out. And then if you don't get rid of her, I will for you.

Alexandro, *shocked, pulls away and leaves. He walks amongst the* **Chorus**.

Dimitra   Don't take him so seriously.

Theo   He doesn't mean it.

Alexandro   He does. He never makes empty threats.

Alexandro *begins to strip off his clothes.* **Eleni** *goes to him.*

Eleni   Alexandro, what are you doing?

Alexandro   Going for a swim.

Eleni   In the middle of the night. You'll catch cold.

Alexandro   You're not my nanny anymore.

Eleni   Oh, I am. Nannies are for life. I still look after you, but at a distance. And you're just the same. You always got upset when you saw him. You still do.

Alexandro   He could harm her.

Eleni   He won't.

Alexandro   But he *could*. Don't put it past him.

Eleni   She loves you. That's all that should matter to you.

Alexandro   That's all that does matter to me. Which is why I'm afraid for her. You know, the first time I ever saw her she was climbing out of a sports car in a snowstorm and I thought she was on fire. But it was just her hair, her incredible red hair, falling on her shoulders like Rome burning. She was the most exciting woman I had ever seen.

Eleni   How old were you then?

Alexandro   Twelve. But I knew what I was doing when I was . . .

Eleni (*laughs*)   Twelve.

Alexandro   Yes. And I suppose being attracted to flames was not surprising with my lineage. I was determined I would marry her when I grew up. And six years later I asked my mother to invite her to a dinner party, and then . . . well, we've not been apart since. Fiona's only three years younger than my mother, so my mother hates her almost as much as my father does, but she's not as dangerous as he is. What's so strange is that she's the only woman I ever really wanted and the only woman I do want and the only woman I ever shall want which of course makes me some sort of a freak, doesn't it, in my father's eyes at least, and in the eyes of his friends and his business associates, and in fact all of society. 'That man will only ever love one woman!' They should put me in a cage in a carnival. It's too confusing. I have to swim. What are you looking at? You've seen me undress so many times.

Eleni   But now you're grown up. You're like a young god.

Alexandro   A lot of good it will do me.

Eleni   Why are you swimming in the middle of the night?

Alexandro   So I can think out loud. It's the one place he can't bug. There are no microphones in the sea.

Alexandro *walks away, into the sea.* **Eleni** *prays.*

Eleni   Poseidon! Do you hear me? Yes, I still believe in you. You're so simple. You're just the sea. Just the huge, unfathomable, unknowable sea. Be gentle with my Alexandro. Don't send one of your sudden midnight storms, don't whip up your waves, don't play games with the tides. Let him swim in calm waters. I am afraid for him.

Costa *prays.*

Costa   My dear Athena, I am no longer certain what Aristo is thinking. He's been in the habit of telling me everything – but suddenly I sense secrets.

Yanni *prays.*

Yanni   Question mark. Why does Mr Onassis want to make financial deals with villains, like the Russians, and the colonels, those little, can I be precise, fascists who have seized control of Greece? Do you know what I'm saying, Hermes? Bear in mind, business only really works if you are able to cheat people you trust. Just kidding.

Theo *prays.*

Theo   The big airlines are in danger, you know – I mean, there are new dangers, not simply the usual problem of falling out of the sky. Now there are bombs and hijackings. People *kidnap* airplanes now. You made a big mistake, almighty Zeus, you forgot to make a god for aviation.

Costa   He is keeping something from me. Perhaps he resents what I have to offer – common sense.

Theo   But listen, here's the genius of Mr Onassis. He has supposedly made a deal with the Palestinians. There's a man in Paris named Hamsari, or Hamshari, or something; he's the PLO's ambassador to France, well, unofficial ambassador, but he's high up and close to Arafat. At least this is the rumour. Mr Onassis has given him a huge payoff – a lot of money – not to hijack our planes. I think that's brilliant. Well, it's just a rumour. It seems you also forgot to make a god for rumours.

Dimitra   Almighty Aphrodite, go away! Who needs a goddess of love? I used to think that love was simple. I never imagined the part that power and possession played. I mean – would Mr Onassis have loved Madame Callas if she hadn't had the most glorious voice in the world? Would he? It doesn't matter that he hates opera, that he says it always sounds like a bunch of Italian chefs screaming risotto recipes at each other. She possessed a commodity that he wanted to own. But now there's a more valuable commodity for sale. And, believe me, that stiffens his penis. I don't understand your world. Fine for you, you're a goddess. But I really don't want to want to speak to you. You and what you represent are unknowable.

Costa (*to audience*)   I imagine Aphrodite has always understood the allure of a private plane. Not to mention that old standby, jewelry. And flowers. For the next four and a half years, Aristo was a very attentive suitor.

Lights rise on **Jackie** *dressing for dinner, watched by* **Aristo**.

Aristo   It doesn't become me.

Jackie   What doesn't?

Aristo   Being a suitor.

Jackie   I would think not. If you want something you take it, don't you?

Aristo   Indeed.

Pause.

The so-called presidential candidate your esteemed brother-in-law suggested I liked to *grab!*

Jackie (*pause*)   I asked him.

Aristo   You what?

Jackie   Asked him.

Aristo   *Asked him?*

Jackie   For permission.

Aristo   You spoke about *us* to that termite, that discarded foreskin, that . . .

Jackie (*laughs*)   Stop it.

Pause.

He's the head of the family. That's a concept you understand. It's very Greek

Aristo   It's not Greek to fuck the head of your family.

Jackie   Oh! You know your mythology better than that.

Aristo   Does he have a tiny prick?

Jackie   He asked the same about you.

Aristo   I would think you gave him an impressive answer.

Jackie (*laughs*)   Do men ever grow up?

Aristo   And what did he say?

Jackie   When?

Aristo   When you asked permission.

Jackie   Oh, he said you can't marry that asshole.

Aristo   What a mundane insult.

Jackie   And I said give me one good reason why not. And he said it would cost him five states. They are the most predictable family in the world. He *says* he needs a Jacqueline Kennedy by his side. How can he run for president standing next to a Jacqueline Onassis? It is, pragmatically, a very good question, although I did point out it would be Ethel by his side, not me, Ethel, the mother of his eighty-three children ... He claimed the voters wouldn't notice her. But of course *I'll* notice her. When she's First Lady. Having dinner parties in *my* house. Does he have any idea how I'll feel? Of course not. He's never thought about it. None of the men in his family have any sensitivity to what a woman actually feels. Jack didn't have a clue, you know. He had no antenna for people and yet total understanding of 'the people'. Sometimes I'd lie awake at night and think how can someone with such global sensitivity be such a shit? Bobby's a bit more complicated. He wants to be a decent person, but his genes won't let him. And yet as a leader of men, he's much more than decent. You figure it out.

Aristo   Why do you continue to sleep with him then?

Jackie   Because it turns you on.

Aristo *bites her finger.*

It does, doesn't it? You don't want to have me, you want to *steal* me.

Pause.

He and I helped each other get through it. Can you understand that?

Aristo   Of course. Grief is famously erotic.

Jackie   Don't be pretentious. Grief is hell.

Aristo   Does Bobby call me 'The Greek?'

Jackie   Yes.

Aristo   I knew that cockroach infested little midget would never call me by my name. Does he lick between your toes, like a cat, as I do ...?

Jackie   Please! He's American, for God's sake.

Pause.

Sometimes I actually manage to feel safe with him.

Pause.

Not *for* him, by the way; I think he's making himself a very easy target. But then I think that men like you and Bobby can excuse your behaviour, even *enjoy* your behaviour, if you know that someday you'll be punished. You are alike, you know. Well, not entirely. You don't share Bobby's distaste for social wrongs. You probably perpetrate them, my dear. You don't care – as he does – about the inequalities of society and the sufferings of the underprivileged. No, don't say anything. It's not your conscience that attracts me. So I asked him how profoundly it would fuck him up if I married you and he said 'Profoundly'. Then I asked if we waited until after the election – would he then give us his blessing. And he said, reluctantly, yes.

Aristo   And you believed him?

Jackie   I don't know. He'll do anything to win an election. Even lie to me. And he does care about me. But you see, he thinks that America has lost something – something *moral* – at its core.

Aristo   Oh, and that two-bit politician, the third and lesser son of the bootlegger, cares about morality?

Jackie   Of course. Don't you understand that that's the contradiction that makes him so attractive? He wants to save his country. What is it you want to save? The problem is he believes that if you really want to change society for the better, you have to be in a position to do so, and he thinks you can only arrive at that position through unethical routes. That's the way it is. So, yes, of course, he would lie to me.

Aristo   As, indeed, I would.

Smiles.

You are in what your Jewish friends call a pickle.

Jackie   Umm . . .

Pause.

I pass myself on magazine covers all the time. I never read the articles. It doesn't matter. I'm trapped, trapped inside other people's words, worse, I'm stuck in my *own* memoir, abandoned in my own life, unable to get the hell out. Can't someone tell me how to get out.

Aristo   You follow the string.

Jackie   And where does it lead?

Aristo   To the one who pulls it.

Bites her ear.

I have secrets that ambulance chaser, that minute scrotum, your little brother-in-law, has never dreamed of. He's an amateur. Follow my string. It leads to freedom. And safety.

Jackie   Safety?

Aristo   Safety for you and your children.

Jackie   Oh.

Aristo   Safety, of course, is expensive. It's a much finer gift than a palace or a ruby, which I will also give to you. But they are replaceable; safety is not.

Kisses her.

Homer was wrong. The siren song was sung by a man.

Starts to make love to her.

The lights fade.

Chorus (*sings*)
> Ksipna mikromou chakouse
> Kasho minore tis avgis
> Gia senane eene grameno
> Apoto klamia kapias psichis
> Gia senane eene grameno
> Apoto klamia kapias psichis

Costa (*to audience*)
> 'Wake up, my little one, and listen
> To a serenade of dawn
> Written especially for you
> Out of a weeping soul ...'

The song is interrupted by gun shots.

Costa   Gunshots again.

Dimitra   *Almost* as famous.

Yanni *runs into* **Aristo***'s office.*

Yanni   I've just heard the news.

Aristo   What news?

Yanni   On the television. Seriously speaking, it's bad news.

Aristo   What news?

Yanni   About Kennedy.

Aristo   What do you mean?

Yanni   Bear in mind, it's not surprising.

Aristo   *Yanni! Tell me the news!*

Yanni   Well, if I may be permitted to say so, someone shot him.

Aristo   Bobby?

Yanni   Yes.

Aristo   Is he dead?

Yanni   I think the specifics of his condition warrant ...

Aristo   Yanni!

Yanni   Yes. He's dead.

Aristo   Who did it?

Yanni   They arrested a young man. A Palestinian.

Aristo   Ah. Palestinian.

Yanni   With a double name. Sirhan. Sirhan. It happened in a hotel. In Los Angeles. In a kitchen. Full stop.

Aristo   Someone was going to fix the little bastard sooner or later.

Aristo *goes to the* **Chorus,** *who begin singing the song he sang at the Kennedy wake.*

Chorus
   Ke pou na rikso
   To megalo mou kaimo
   Opou na aniksi I gis
   Ke tha raisi to vouno
   Ilie fonia posa fises na gini to kako
   Skotosane to *stavraeto* Ke ton avgerino
   Kato stostavro dromi skotasane tonio

Aristo   I sang that song to him in Washington. He disliked it. And now you sing it *for* him? He also disliked irony. He doesn't know what he missed. I must phone Jackie and offer my condolences. She's free of them now. The Kennedys. The last link just broke. I imagine this time I *won't* be invited to the funeral.

Aristo *walks away.*

Dimitra (*to* **Costa**)   Your hero? In the classics, when an enemy dies, the heroes are humble.

Costa   He may be many things, but he is *not* a hypocrite!

Dimitra   Poor Madame Callas.

Yanni   Why?

Dimitra   He can marry the other one now.

Alexandro *enters*.

Alexandro   He mustn't. He mustn't marry her.

Eleni   It's not your place to say.

Alexandro   She just wants his money.

Theo   He says that about *your* girlfriend.

Alexandro   I hear she's asked for twenty million dollars up front.

Dimitra   She could price herself out of the market.

Yanni   She'll get three million plus one million for each of her children, if I may say so thank heaven there are only two, and Ari will be responsible for her expenses as long as the marriage lasts. And after his death 150,000 dollars a year for life. That's his offer. End of paragraph.

Theo   They will compromise.

Costa   They both understand that the shame of the market is not in being sold, but undersold.

Yanni   Bear in mind, corporate mergers are always difficult.

Alexandro   If there's a wedding, I won't go to it.

Eleni   Why do you care so much what your father does?

Alexandro   I don't. I don't give a damn. I hate him.

Pause.

I worry about him. Even the singer was better than this.

Alexandro *leaves*. **Aristo** *leads* **Jackie** *into his garden*.

Aristo   My island is shaped like a scorpion. So it is called Skorpios. At first the island was covered only with olive trees. I've added all the trees of the Bible – almonds, bramble, pine, oleander, figs. I planted many of them myself. My grandmother taught me all I know about things that grow. Did you know the fig is the first of the fruits to be mentioned in the Old Testament? To sit beneath one's own fig tree was the Jewish ideal of peace and prosperity. Look at this – a pine cone. My grandmother said if you cut it lengthwise, it resembles the hand of Jesus. All the Turkish Greeks knew things like that. Exile thrives on mythology. Still – there are mysteries in nature, aren't there?

Jackie   I suppose.

Aristo   And now the island will be yours as well.

Jackie   Joint ownership of fig trees?

Jackie *walks to a pool of water that sits at the front of the stage.* **Aristo** *goes to her.*

Aristo   What are you thinking?

Jackie   That life has so many unexpected turns. And twists. And curves.

Pause.

Fig trees.

Pause.

I shall like it here.

Jackie *and* **Aristo** *walk off slowly.*

Chorus

Mikros aravoniastika
Koroido pou piastika
Ke pira mia bebeka mariola gia gineka
Ke pira mia bebeka mariola gia gineka
Sto ygamo magana souna
Na vlepesti iche giini
San namouna ipodi kos ke berimeno diki san namouna
ipodikos keperimeno diki

Dimitra *(watching from the side)*   Poor Madame Callas.

Maria *enters.*

Maria   I do not feel betrayed.

Pause.

They have every right to make their own decisions and to follow their own paths.

Pause.

Let me hear my voice.

Desperately – to the darkness.

My voice!

Callas singing 'Casta Diva' floods the stage. **Maria** *listens and begins to weep.*

What was it about? How could I have been in touch with the gods? Apollo, oh Apollo, why did you choose me? Did you just look down from the sky and say 'Oh look, there's a fat Greek girl, let's give her a gift from heaven. All she wants to eat is chocolate and cake, but no, let her have ambrosia, in her throat, nectar from Olympus, let her have the voice of an angel, let her larynx be a lyre, a flute, a violin, let all of the ugliness of life dissolve when she opens her mouth, let her give pleasure to a despairing human race, like one of those creatures who distracted Odysseus from returning home, let her make a sound that might shipwreck sailors, a sound so beautiful and sometimes so ugly at the same time that it could not possibly be mortal.' Oh blessed Apollo, I didn't want it, don't you understand, I did not want it. But once you gave it to me, I had to become a high priestess, I had to guard the flame. You charged me to never let the flame die. I watched the flame flicker and fade and I did nothing because I had found my own siren song and it was sung by a cruel man in dark glasses.

Pause.

You have punished me, Apollo, and now all I yearn for is death. But you are a god, and surely you understand vengeance. Then give me my vengeance. Punish him! Do

you hear me, Apollo, punish him! My dearest Ari, my love,
my life, my fire, my *man*, I curse you, I curse you and I
curse everyone who touches you, and I call upon the gods
to hear me. Hear me, Apollo, hear my curse! Once I could
have sung it, I could have stood in an opera house and sung
my curse, and it would have been the most beautiful curse
in the world, and people would have cried and grabbed
each other and carried memories of my curse for the rest of
their wretched lives, but now I can only speak it,
pathetically, brokenly, in a voice that will no longer give you
pleasure, but, nonetheless, hear it!

Falls to her knees.

If you still call yourself a god, if you still have any power at
all, if you still control man's fate, then listen to my plea and
... destroy him!

Suddenly – silence. **Maria** *rises and regains her composure.*

Maria   I wish them nothing but happiness.

Starts to leave.

Dimitra   You are in such pain.

Maria   Of course not. I am perfectly alright.

Dimitra   But you are suffering.

Maria   Nonsense. I am at peace with myself.

Dimitra   Please, don't leave. Stay with us.

Maria   With you?

Dimitra (*puts her arms around* **Maria**)   We can comfort you.

Maria   Thank you.

Moves away.

But I can't.

Dimitra   Why not?

Maria   You're the *chorus!*

Maria *leaves. The* **Chorus** *start to sing a wedding song.*

Chorus
  Mikros aravoniastika
  Koroido pou piastika
  Ke pira mia bebeka mariola gia gineka
  Ke pira mia bebeka mariola gia gineka
  Sto ygamo magana souna
  Na vlepesti iche giini
  San namouna ipodi kos ke berimeno diki san namouna
  ipodikos keperimeno diki

Dimitra (*to audience, in middle of song*)
  I was like a man in custody,
  Awaiting trial.
  And then the verdict was announced –
  I was married!

Aristo *walks in, a drink in hand, very drunk. He continues the song with them.*

Dimitra   You join us on your wedding night?

Aristo   Of course. Am I not the son of the people?

Dimitra *raises an eyebrow, to the audience.*

Aristo (*pouring a drink from a bottle, then hands the bottle to* **Costa**)   Another drink? My wife is asleep. She's not a fan of carousing. Luckily, we had our honeymoon night several hours before the marriage ceremony.

Dimitra   Shame on you. To see your bride before the ceremony on the day of the wedding is tempting fate.

Aristo   Ah, fate. Ah yes. Fate.

Pause.

My wife has cost me a lot.

Costa   You did make a considerable settlement.

Aristo   I'm not talking about money. I'm talking about my *soul!*

Costa   Don't exaggerate.

Aristo   I'm not. My soul, Costa, my soul. Do you know who owns it?

Costa   Who?

Aristo   Hamshari.

To the **Others**.

Leave me, please.

Aristo *puts his hand on* **Costa***'s shoulder, and motions for him and* **Yanni** *to stay, as* **Dimitra**, **Eleni**, **Theo** *and the* **Musicians** *leave.*

Aristo   Gentlemen, I believe I told you that I had paid Mohmoud Hamshari 350,000 US dollars as protection money. I wasn't quite telling you the truth. I have actually agreed to pay him 1.2 million dollars.

Yanni   One-point-two? That's, I would like to say, an exorbitant amount of money.

Aristo   It is. Yes.

Yanni   But if I may call it a spade. That's practically extortion.

Aristo   It *is* extortion. Yanni. That's the point. Alright. That's all. You will have to do some creative accounting. It was on my mind. I wanted you to know. Goodnight.

Yanni *hesitates, then leaves.*

Costa   So. You *have* been keeping secrets.

Aristo   Sometimes I must. Even from you. Tonight this bothers me. But it will pass. I'm suddenly sober. I hate that. And I drank so much. Pity.

Costa   There's more.

Aristo   More what?

Costa   One-point-two million dollars, Aristo?

Aristo   This Mr Hamshari. He does his homework. As you
know, I appreciate that. I suppose we have a lot in common.
Exile and a desire for revenge.

Pours another drink.

Costa   And?

Aristo   I can't even call this a *drunken* confession. I'm so
fucking alert. Well – he had told me about an idea of his.
Evidently after the Six Day War he proposed to the
Palestinian leadership that they assassinate a prominent
American. A kind of wake-up call to America, to dissuade
them from supporting Israel. Crazy, isn't it?

Costa   Crazy.

Aristo   Well, everyone thought it was crazy, even Arafat; he
thought Hamshari was a loose canon and packed him off to
Paris. Did you know any of this?

Costa   Obviously not.

Aristo   Umm. You're slipping. I thought you had *sources.*
Anyhow, Hamshari still wanted to proceed with his plan and
he asked me to finance it.

Costa   Aristo . . . !

Aristo   You can't start being shocked by me now, my dear,
not after all these years. He wrote the name on a piece of
paper. He *had* done his homework. He knew how much I
hated.

Costa   And?

Aristo   Hence 1.2 million dollars. Far more than the price
of protection against hijackers.

Costa   I see.

Aristo   It wasn't just revenge. It was expediency as well.
Bobby would never have allowed her to marry me. He told
her to wait until after the elections, but he was simply
stalling for time. Hamshari said he could arrange for

someone to carry it off. Some poor sap, someone they could brainwash – whatever. I wasn't to be concerned about the particulars. I was actually surprised it happened. I thought I had thrown my money away. And I most certainly don't regret it, that little cocksucker had it coming. But it does take a rather prominent place in my thoughts, on this evening, the evening of my marriage. I did, after all, pay for the murder of possibly the only man my wife ever really loved. The odd thing is it makes me desire her more.

Costa   Of course you don't know ...

Aristo   Don't know?

Costa   If he really used the money to carry out that particular operation. He might have simply pocketed the money for himself. That event ... that unfortunate event might have had nothing to do with you.

Aristo   Are you implying I was conned?

Costa   Well – we'll never know, will we?

Pause.

So why are you so worried?

Aristo   Is that one of your wise little questions? I hate it when you pretend to know me. Go to sleep. I'm not worried. Not in the least.

Pause.

I would just be slightly more comfortable if it were a secret.

Costa   A secret?

Aristo   Well, if it hadn't been overheard; my conversation with Hamshari, that is.

Costa   But who could possibly have heard it?

Aristo   The gods, my friend, the gods.

Blackout.

Act Two

The **Chorus** *sit at the taverna, with the* **Musicians**.

Chorus (*sing*)
    Argo to vima mes ti nich-ta
    Me tin gavega varia va dizo
    Figaneoliu ke m'afisan
    Na peri meno kapio dilino
    Monogia me nane karavi
    Den echi pia na taksidepso
    Keta limania ke I katha
    Keri ka die mafisa ekso

Alexandro *walks through the* **Chorus**, *a manila envelope in his hand.*

Alexandro   You're as bad as my father. You can turn everything into rebetiko.

Dimitra   You don't believe in bouzouki nights?

Alexandro   Singing, dancing, drinking, breaking dishes, Melina, Zorba. No, I don't believe in it. Anyhow, there is nothing to celebrate. My aunt Eugenia is dead.

Costa (*to audience*)   That's Eugenia, wife of Stavros Niarchos, sister to Tina, former wife of Aristotle ...

Yanni   Please – don't start again.

Alexandro   My family are all mad; they're killing each other ...

Eleni   You mustn't get carried away ...

Alexandro   I'm not. I'm perfectly calm.

Costa (*to audience*)   Niarchos, if you remember, is sleeping with his wife's sister, Tina, the former wife of ...

Dimitra   *Will you stop that!!!!*

Alexandro   Everyone talks about my family, and yet none of us know the truth.

Aristo *enters and goes into his office;* **Alexandro** *follows him.*

Aristo   I'm ordering more eucalyptus trees for the island. I like the way the perfume of the eucalyptus trees mingles with the smell of the salt.

Alexandro   What salt?

Aristo   From the sea, what do you think? You're so linear. You have no poetry. What the fuck do you want?

Alexandro   You're in a good mood today.

Aristo (*picks up some papers*)   Have you seen these? Bills! Dresses!

Alexandro   Are you wearing dresses now?

Aristo   Don't be a smart ass. I married a walking credit card. Don't say anything. What are you doing here?

Alexandro   You have the goods on Stavro, don't you?

Aristo   What?

Alexandro   Uncle Stavro.

Aristo   I hate it when you call him that. You know, in ancient Greek, eucalyptus means well-covered. An interesting term. Not necessarily applicable to your *Uncle* Stavro anymore.

Alexandro   You have tapes of phone conversations, don't you?

Aristo   Why don't you come and help me plant them? Work up a sweat for a change. You're becoming effete.

Alexandro   You have tapes. You bugged his house and you have tapes.

Aristo   You're repeating yourself. That woman of yours is making you senile. You need a charge account at Madame Claude's. The trouble with you is you've never paid for it. Yes, I have transcripts. The eucalyptus, like most of my trees, is mentioned in the Bible, did you know that?

Alexandro   I don't care about trees!

Aristo   You should! You should love the earth!

Alexandro   Look – everyone thinks Stavro was somehow responsible for Aunt Eugenia's death, even though he's never been charged. You have every word he spoke on the phone that night carefully *recorded*, don't you? And I assume it trashes his alibi.

Aristo   You have a one-track mind, which is fine, but you have to learn to hide it sometimes.

Alexandro   What will you do with the tapes?

Aristo   I haven't decided. I have so many delicious choices. What's important is that after all these years, *I have him! Your Uncle Stavro*. How do you know all of this?

Alexandro   Mother. She took my sister to lunch. And she gave this to her. Here.

Hands him the envelope.

Aristo   What is it?

Alexandro   Open it.

Aristo   Don't you dare give me orders.

Alexandro   Oh, please. Just open it.

Aristo   From your mother?

Alexandro   Yes.

Aristo   It might explode.

Alexandro *stares at him.*

Aristo   Alright, alright. You want to be serious. Be serious.

He opens the envelope. He takes out some papers and glances at them.

Alexandro   Conversations you've had with Costa. They have, of course, taped you too. These are the transcripts.

And you know that poor patsy, the one who pulled the
trigger, Sirhan Sirhan, left notebooks behind. There's a
copy of some fragments from one of those notebooks here.
The name Fiona is scrawled on one page. Fiona! Demented
Mid-Eastern assassins don't usually speak the name Fiona,
let alone write it in a notebook. And, on another page,
there's the name Niarchos, spelled wrong, but still
unmistakable. What did you do, make some kind of package
deal? Were you going to have them killed as well? I mean,
are you totally mad? Where do you live – in some kind of
malevolent never-never land?

Aristo   Your mother gave these to you?

Alexandro   You may have him, but it seems that he has
you as well.

Aristo   Your mother actually asked you to read these?

Alexandro   Doesn't matter. Those are copies. I've put the
originals in a safe. If anything happens to Fiona – do you
understand me? – if you ever dare harm her – I will expose
you.

Aristo   How could she allow you to read this? You have to
forget all about this.

Alexandro   Maybe you're not following me. I've put the
originals in a safe deposit box.

Aristo   You must wipe this from your mind. And never,
ever mention it to anyone.

Alexandro   Who am I going to tell? 'Hi, did you know my
father paid for the murder of Robert Kennedy? You know –
daddy – the tree planter – lover of the earth.' How about
your wife? Maybe I should tell her? Well, I will tell her if
Fiona is hurt. You understand me?

Aristo   Your mother is a selfish bitch.

Alexandro   That's neither here nor there.

Aristo   I don't know how she could do this to you.

Alexandro   You're the one doing, not her. Fiona is the woman I love and you want to kill her.

Aristo   Doesn't your mother care about you?

Alexandro   This has nothing to do with mother. Why are you fixating on her?

Aristo   *Because you mustn't know these things!* Because it's dangerous. Knowledge is dangerous. At least when you're swimming in this kind of sea. Too many people, too many factions, too many secrets. You must stay out of this. It's not your world.

Alexandro   No it's not. Thank God for that. OK, I've warned you.

Aristo   No. *I've* warned *you.*

Alexandro   Right, then. We're even.

Pause.

What will you do with the tapes?

Aristo (*shrugs*)   Bury them, I suppose. Next to the eucalyptus. And await the next round.

Alexandro   I will never understand you.

Alexandro *leaves, and walks to the* **Chorus**.

Costa   You know what your father would say?

Alexandro   What?

Costa   Understanding is overrated.

Alexandro   He's grotesque. Whenever I'm with him, I can hear my heart pumping. I keep waiting for someone to ask 'What's that terrible noise?' But no one else can hear it.

Eleni   Yes, you've always loved him.

Alexandro   He would have killed Fiona.

Eleni   And he's always loved you.

Alexandro   Fiona's building a house in Switzerland. When it's ready I'll move in with her. I'll go to university. I'll get a degree. I'll get a job. I'll walk away. Just watch me.

Aristo *enters, drunk, holding a liquor bottle and a glass.*

Aristo   Are you still here?

Alexandro   I'm leaving.

Alexandro *leaves.*

Aristo   He always says 'I'm leaving'. Usually as he's arriving. Why aren't you singing? How about gel kaiksi?

Dimitra   If you like.

Sings.
   Gel, gel kaiksi
   Gia vas, gia vas
   Mes tis polis t'akrogiali
   Mes ti sigalia

Aristo, *who is getting drunk, and the* **Chorus**, *join her.*

Aristo and **Chorus** (*sing*)
   Mes tou caremiou
   Ti lithi
   Gel, gel kaksis

Jackie *enters. She carries a book.*

Jackie   What are you singing?

Aristo   What does it matter?

Jackie   I'd like to know. It's beautiful.

Aristo (*mimics her voice*)   It's beautiful.

Jackie   Yanni, you're looking very chipper today.

Yanni   Thank you. The song is about a boat.

Jackie   A boat?

Costa   Yes. A caique.

Jackie   Oh. That's a beautiful shirt, by the way, Costa.

Eleni   From Turkey.

Jackie   The shirt?

Eleni   No. The caique.

Jackie   Oh. Sorry. I love the way you're always so direct, Eleni. It's an admirable quality.

Eleni   Thank you, Mrs Onassis.

Jackie   The children appreciated the apricot cake. They thought it delicious.

Eleni (*beams*)   Thank you, Mrs Onassis.

Aristo   This is making me sick.

Theo   The song is also about the owner of the caique.

Jackie   Oh. A ship-owner!

Theo   Well, no, it's just a caique.

Jackie   Oh, small beans, then. But quite a different world than aviation, isn't it, Theo?

She flashes him her most radiant smile.

Dimitra   It's the owner who is singing.

Jackie   And, Dimitra, did I thank you for the flower arrangements on the yacht last week? They were very tastefully done.

Dimitra   Were they?

Jackie   Oh yes. You have a 'touch'.

Dimitra (*blushes*)   I like flowers.

Jackie   And what is it that the owner is singing?

Dimitra
  'Let's steal the beautiful woman,
  A slave in her own cell.
  She cries and grieves
  And asks for her freedom …'

Jackie   Oh.

Dimitra   Do you like it?

Jackie (*smiles*)   'A slave in her own cell?'

Dimitra   Yes.

Jackie (*to* **Aristo**, *pointing to the liquor*)   May I have some?

Aristo (*pours her a glass*)   Don't drink *too* much. You're hardly a slave, you know.

Jackie   I never said I was.

Drinks.

Aristo   Slaves don't spend 30,000 dollars a month on clothing.

Jackie   That's overstated. Although I *am* high maintenance. You knew that.

Holds out her glass for another.

Aristo   Yes, well, that was always one of my weaknesses, paying for sex.

Jackie   An admirable one.

Aristo   The problem is sleeping with you is like fucking an ironing board.

Jackie (*a long pause*)   What would you know . . .

Longer pause.

. . . about an ironing board?

Aristo (*amused*)   Almost as little as you, I admit.

Jackie   Anyhow, it's not true. You once told me I was like a diamond – 'cool and sharp at the edges, fiery and hot beneath the surface'.

Laughs.

Who's to argue?

Stands very close to him.

Do you like my perfume?

Aristo   I should. It probably cost twenty thousand.

Jackie   Ten. There was a sale.

Aristo   All that money on clothing and yet whenever I see you you're wearing jeans.

Jackie   Well my clothes are too nice to wear. That's a subtlety that has to do with market value; I thought you would appreciate it.

Aristo   I loathe subtlety.

Jackie   You're named after two masters of subtlety.

Aristo   What do you know about Aristotle or Socrates? You read an article about them? Don't talk to me about philosophers. *Greek* philosophers! Go away! I can't bear the sight of you.

Jackie (*laughs, holds out her glass*)   More, please.

Aristo   I thought marrying you would give me class.

Pours her another drink.

Jackie   There's no such thing. Not in our world, darling. It's like morality – it's a moveable feast. You have it and you don't, both at the same time.

Aristo   The whole fucking planet is angry at me because I married you.

Jackie   I know, they think you're a promiscuous scoundrel. But you're my *second* promiscuous scoundrel. No one cared the first time. Maybe you should have married Maria.

Pause.

I know you're seeing Maria again. Do you know what upsets me?

Aristo   I don't care.

Jackie It upsets me that you are photographed in public. The whole point of infidelity used to be that it was secret.

Pause.

I'll tell you what I would like more than anything. A quiet evening. Just the two of us, talking, or, nicer still, not talking. Reading. Sitting across from each other, reading, together. Think about it.

To **Chorus**.

Talk to him, my friends. Tell him he could have done much worse.

Jackie *leaves.*

Theo *leaves shortly after.*

Dimitra I hate to admit it, but she's right.

Costa Why don't you have that quiet evening?

Aristo Yes. In theory that would be nice.

Pause.

I can't.

Pause.

Anyhow, it's not my style. When have I ever had a *quiet* evening? She's trying to divert my attention. She knows I've been speaking to lawyers. About a divorce. It's tricky. Ever since I married her my most promising business deals have fallen apart. Beneath all the couturier clothing lies an evil eye. Of course, it might be different if she would deign to appear by my side at a business dinner. A Jacqueline Kennedy is a desirable consort when closing a deal. Well, I suppose it was a fantasy. . . . And now just think of the kind of settlement she will demand. You know, basically, people only know three things about me: I'm fucking Jackie Kennedy, I'm fucking Maria Callas and I'm fucking rich.

Takes **Costa** *aside.*

Did you hear about Hamshari?

Costa   Of course. He was blown up . . .

Aristo   Answering his telephone.

Costa   By the Israelis. But evidently he didn't die. He's in hospital making a remarkable recovery.

Aristo   Not *that* remarkable. He developed a mysterious fever last night and now he's *really* dead. This time it was his own side that did him in. Supposedly. You can never tell, when it comes to that part of the world, who's killing who. Poor Hamshari knew too much. That's not a phrase I enjoy, my friend. *He knew too much.* I've dreamt about him, at least I think I have, I don't even remember what he looked like. I can see him reaching for the fucking telephone. My nose for danger wasn't twitching enough, was it? What was I thinking?

To **Dimitra***.*

You didn't translate all of the song, did you? There's a line about 'the oblivion of the harem'. Hah! 'Come, come caique owner!'

Sings.
   Gel, gel kaiksi
   Yia vas, yia vas . . .

Theo, *who had walked offstage; returns with a wire in his hand.*

Theo   Mr Onassis, there's been an accident. Your private jet crashed on the way to the island.

Aristo   Who was on board?

Theo   Just Dimitri and Giorgio, the pilots.

Dimitra   *Just?*

Aristo   And?

Theo   They're dead.

Aristo *registers this for a moment in silence, then turns to* **Costa***.*

Aristo   It must have been sabotage.

Costa   Let's wait and find out.

Aristo   They're trying to kill me.

Costa   Who are 'they'?

Aristo   Does it matter?

Aristo *leaves.* **Alexandro** *enters, agitated.*

Alexandro   No one knows what went wrong. Some people heard an explosion.

Eleni   The gods are unhappy.

Alexandro   I've been flying over the sea looking for wreckage.

Eleni   You should stay away from airplanes.

Alexandro   You don't understand. They were my friends. They taught me how to fly.

Dimitra   In olden days if something fell from the sky it would have been a sign.

Aristo *enters and draws* **Alexandro** *to him and embraces him.*

Aristo   Life goes in cycles. I should never have married her. I might have overplayed my hand. I have enemies everywhere. When you have enemies, there's no such thing as an accident.

Alexandro   Wait a minute, you don't think this has something to do with Kennedy ...

Aristo   Don't say it. It's not something we speak about. You know that. The walls have ears.

Alexandro   Look, this isn't *your* tragedy. This was an accident and I've lost two friends.

Aristo   I know, I know, it's difficult the first time you lose a friend. But it's part of growing up. You get used to it.

You've never had to live through a war. You never had the Turks ...

Alexandro   Please, don't tell me about Smyrna again.

Aristo   Listen, you brat, I'm trying to teach you something.

Alexandro   I've just heard those stories, over and over ...

Aristo   A parent is supposed to repeat himself. That's what we do! Why can't you ever ...

Alexandro   OK. I'm sorry.

Aristo   What?

Alexandro   I said I'm sorry.

Aristo   Oh.

Pause.

I am too.

Alexandro   You're what?

Aristo   What you said.

Alexandro   Which was?

Aristo   You know damn well.

Alexandro   What did I say?

Aristo   You said you were sorry and I said I was sorry. OK. Are you happy now?

Alexandro (*smiles*)   What are we sorry about?

Aristo   *It doesn't fucking matter!* Jesus! Go away. You get on my nerves.

Alexandro   OK, pop.

Starts to leave.

Aristo   Wait!

Alexandro   What now?

Aristo   OK. Alright. It's yours.

Alexandro   What's mine?

Aristo   The Puma.

Alexandro   Puma?

Aristo   The helicopter you asked me for.

Alexandro   Oh. I asked you last year.

Aristo   And I'm giving it this year.

Alexandro   Why?

Aristo   Who knows? I'm kind. That old amphibian, the Piaggio, it's ancient, you're right, we need a new one, it's a present, don't you dare thank me.

Alexandro   I wasn't going to.

Aristo   I'm not completely detached from human emotion, you know. I understand loss. And when you lose something, it's nice to have something else in return.

Alexandro   I don't believe this. I lost two *friends* . . .

Aristo   So you say.

Alexandro   You don't replace people with . . .

Aristo   What? *Things?* Oh go away. You have your mother's eyes.

Alexandro   Is that good or bad?

Aristo   It just is.

Kisses **Alexandro** *on the lips.*

It's not that you're stupid, I don't think that, it's rather that you're . . . dumb.

Alexandro   I don't want your gift.

Aristo   So don't take it.

He stares at **Alexandro**.

Alexandro *knows he has lost.*

Aristo *throws him the keys to the Puma.* **Alexandro** *grabs them and walks off.*

Aristo *goes to the* **Chorus**.

Aristo   What do you think? He's not so bad. He talks back. I never talked back to my father. I spent weeks searching for my family. I thought they were dead. I did make my way to Constantinople, however, with whatever I could salvage of the family fortune bandaged to my body. It was the first time I was ever alone. I recognised then that 'alone' was a condition of survival. And so I have remained ever since – does that surprise you? – despite the innumerable people who surround me and depend on me and even, in their pedestrian imaginations, 'love' me. Anyhow, I found out my old man was alive and bribed the right people – and sprang him from prison. He never thanked me. For saving his life! That was my first lesson in futility.

Pause.

Sssh, do you hear it?

Costa   What?

Aristo   Quiet. Quiet's not healthy. I'm uneasy.

Costa   What about?

Aristo   Haven't a clue.

Pause.

I've never waited for anything in my life. And now I am. I'm waiting.

Looks up at sky.

They're waiting too.

Walks off.

Theo   The sky is grey. A Greek sky should be blue.

Eleni   Poseidon hasn't sent a wind from the sea.

Dimitra   Apollo has hidden the sun with clouds.

Yanni   But there is no rain.

Costa   Wherever you look you can see – nothing.

Eleni   He's right. The gods are waiting.

Dimitra   Let them wait. Nothing is certain except for this – the gods will fuck you up.

Yanni *walks off.*

Alexandro *encounters* **Jackie**.

Alexandro   Oh.

Jackie   Oh?

Alexandro   Excuse me.

Jackie   Yes?

Alexandro   Father?

Jackie   Office.

Alexandro   Oh.

Jackie   Oh?

Pause.

Alexandro   Tell him I'm taking the Piaggio out one more time.

Jackie   That's nice.

Alexandro   Then it's onto the scrapheap.

Jackie   The Piaggio?

Alexandro   Yes.

Pause.

Jackie   This has been the longest conversation we've ever had. Not to mention the deepest.

Alexandro   It doesn't matter anymore.

Jackie   Why not?

Alexandro   You're heading for the scrapheap as well.

Jackie   Are you so certain?

Alexandro   Don't worry. He'll make a reasonable settlement.

Jackie   Do you think it's only the money I care about?

Alexandro   What else?

Jackie   Well – it's exciting, don't you think? The contradictions. The uncertainty. Treading on quicksand. Monsters attract me. Their mouths are dripping with blood because they've been devouring life – uncooked. They're a dying breed, you know. I meet the new ones now, the up and comers. The ones who are primed for power, the ones who will take over their organisations, their parties and ultimately their countries. They're faithful to their wives – honestly, can you imagine? – they're patriotic, they believe in God – one god, I might add, not the interesting variety that some of you still take seriously – and they are possibly even bearable parents. They may be rather similar to you. And yet, underneath, they're as empty and, I imagine, corrupt – and dangerous certainly – as the powerful always are. Perhaps more dangerous, because they always know they're right, unlike my first husband and his brother, who at least flirted with doubt; and they think too that they have values, unlike your father, who knows he possesses nothing of the kind. But he is peanut butter chocolate laced with rum and strawberries. Whereas the future is vanilla. You should appreciate him while you can.

Pause.

Alexandro   I do.

Pause.

Jackie   Good.

Pause.

Alexandro   Tell him I was here.

Jackie   Alright.

Pause.

You don't happen to know, do you ... I mean ... has he ever mentioned to you ... the *size* of the settlement?

Alexandro *smiles and leaves. He walks through the* **Chorus**.

Eleni   Where are you going?

Alexandro   Back to Athens.

Eleni   Why?

Alexandro   I'm taking the Piaggio out for one last flight.

Eleni   Do you have to?

Alexandro (*kisses her forehead*)   Yes. I'm actually going to miss it.

Alexandro *leaves.*

Dimitra (*sings*)
  Sto pepromeno sou na dinis simasia
  Ken a prosechis pos vadizis sti zoi
  Otan kimase alos grafi istoria
  Ke kapios pezi ti diki sou dip sichi

  Olie chou me grameno
  Pou to lene pepromeno
  Kekannas na sve borina tapo fiyi
  Den I parchi theoria
  Outre trena oute plia
  Kio kathenas to palevi opas kseri
  (Ke bori Apopedi
  Stonipnnomou evlepaoties)

A hesitant **Yanni** *goes to* **Aristo**, *who is studying papers at his desk.*

Aristo   Yes, Yanni?

Silence. **Aristo** *looks up, but clearly doesn't want to be distracted.*

Aristo   What is it?

Silence.

Say something.

Yanni   Let me put it this way, McCusker was going to replace McGregor.

Aristo   Pardon?

Yanni   Well, to rephrase it, McGregor was going to show him how.

Aristo   Sorry?

Yanni   McCusker.

Aristo   Have *you* had a stroke?

Yanni   Your pilot. Donald McGregor.

Aristo   Yes. My pilot. I *know* he's my pilot.

Yanni   And he's leaving.

Aristo   Yes. I know he's leaving.

Yanni   And Donald McCusker is replacing him.

Aristo   So?

Yanni   So now it's clear what I'm saying.

Pause.

I think I'll leave.

Starts to go.

Aristo   Yanni!

Yanni   Yes sir?

Turns back.

Aristo   What do you want to tell me?

Yanni   I don't *want* to tell you anything. But, bear in mind, they are both named Donald.

Aristo   *Who* are?

Yanni   McGregor and McCusker.

Aristo   I'm going mad.

Yanni   It's a coincidence, isn't it? Luck. Two Donalds.
Perhaps it has some meaning ...

Aristo   Yanni!!

Yanni   Well – perhaps not.

Aristo (*puts his papers down and concentrates on* **Yanni**)   Yanni!
You are unequalled at figures. That's why I keep you. Do
you understand? It's the *only* reason I keep you. People
think me intolerant. You prove that I am not. Still, you are
an endlessly boring man. Now I want you to take a deep
breath – obviously you are upset and you need to calm
down a bit. Alright? Breathe deeply ... yes. Now try to
construct a few simple sentences. And get to the fucking
point.

Yanni   Yes, sir. The point.

Aristo   The point.

Yanni   They went out with Alexandro.

Aristo   Oh? (*suddenly nervous*)   Alexandro?

Yanni   Yes, sir.

Aristo   They?

Yanni   McGregor and McCusker, yes. Donald and Donald,
as it were. Out. Full stop.

Aristo   Alexandro ...

Yanni   On the Piaggia.

Aristo   Alexandro!

Yanni   McCusker had never flown one and McGregor
wanted to show him.

Aristo   And Alexandro?

Yanni   Oh, he wanted, in a manner of speaking, to quote
the boy himself, one last flight.

Aristo (*quietly*)   I think you better tell me.

Yanni   Yes, they said to tell you. But it's easy enough for them to say that . . .

Aristo   Listen to me very carefully. I want you to say what it is. I'm not going to be angry with you, I promise I won't hurt you . . .

Yanni   Alright, may I just inform you . . .

Aristo   Quickly!!!

Yanni   There was, may I say, engine failure.

Aristo   *Engine* failure?

Yanni   The plane lost its balance, that's all and then suddenly it, if I may use this word, dropped.

Aristo   Dropped?

Yanni   From the sky.

Aristo (*softly*)   And my son?

Yanni   I think you should perhaps speak to the . . .

Aristo   *My son?*

Yanni   . . . hospital. Yes, they will notify you at the hospital.

Aristo   *Notify?*

Yanni   Well, present you with the particulars . . . the specifics . . . the . . . (*Cannot bear the look on* **Aristo**'s *face*.) . . . the fact is, if I may put it this way, Alexandro's not . . . not still . . .

Aristo   He's dead.

Pause.

Yanni   Yes.

Pause.

Aristo   I see. Thank you, Yanni. You can go now.

Yanni *hesitates.*

Aristo   I've kept my promise. Go.

Yanni *starts to leave.* **Aristo** *suddenly lunges at him and grabs his throat.*

Aristo   Liar!

Aristo *is strangling* **Yanni**.

Aristo   Fucking liar! Son of a whore! How dare you make up stories about my son!

Costa *and* **Theo** *run in and pull* **Aristo** *off* **Yanni**.

Costa   Aristo . . .

Aristo   My child. They have killed my child.

Costa   Aristo, Alexandro is amongst the angels now.

Aristo   What the hell good will that do him?

He waves the still-terrified **Yanni** *away and pulls himself together.*

Aristo   Someone will have to notify his sister. And his mother. And, I suppose, his woman.

Takes **Costa**'s *hand.*

You know, Costa, there are probably millions of people in the world at this very moment crossing themselves and saying 'Thank God, I am not Onassis'.

Pause.

Thank God I am not Onassis!

He opens his mouth – an enlongated, strangulated scream comes out. He starts offstage; **Costa** *and* **Theo** *try to help him, but he pushes them away.* **Dimitra** *starts to sing a piercing lament that turns into the song* **Aristo** *sung at the Kennedy wake.*

Dimitra (*sings*)
   Ke pou na rikso
   To megalo mou kaimo
   Opou na aniksi I gis
   Ke tha raisi to vouno

Dimitra and **Eleni** (*sing*)
  Ilie fonia posa fises na gini to kako
  Skotosane to *stavraeto* Ke ton avgerino
  Kato stostavro dromi skotasane tonio

Eleni *almost faints;* **Yanni** *props her up.*

Costa (*to audience*)
  'They killed the golden eagle
  The morning star
  Down in the crossroad
  They killed the bright young man'. . .

Theo   'The golden eagle'. 'The morning star'. Why do we always sing about *special* people? Why do we mourn 'the bright young man'? Not every young man is a prince. Is the death of a golden eagle more tragic than that of a pigeon?

Dimitra   They both shit on your head.

Eleni (*reviving*)   We all knew it was his destiny, didn't we? Don't say we didn't.

Yanni   If we can't blame the gods, where does that leave us?

Aristo *returns, with a bottle and an envelope. He drinks.*

Aristo (*to* **Chorus**)   Well, what do you think? Tell me. Do you really believe it was an accident? Do you?

Dimitra   I'm afraid accidents happen, Mr Onassis. They are beyond our control.

Aristo   Oh really? Who asked you? No, there are too many questions. Too many unsolved mysteries. Why did a plane fall out of the sky on a perfect winter afternoon? I have a report from the Air Force –

Holds out envelope.

Here – read it. Reversed cables. That's what they found. The cables in the plane were each on the wrong side. Well, come on, read it.

Thrusts papers at them.

Who reversed them? Who wanted to kill my Alexandro? Who hated my Alexandro?

Theo   I don't think anyone hated him. He was a fine young man.

Aristo   Yes, he was.

Theo   Everyone loved him.

Aristo   Yes. Thank you, my friend.

Takes a big wad of cash out of his pocket.

Everyone loved him. Here.

Shows the money to **Theo**.

Buy yourself something.

He tries to give **Theo** *the cash;* **Theo** *resists.*

Costa   Aristo!

Aristo   No, no, take it.

Thrusts the money into **Theo**'s *hand.*

It's only money. What does money matter? Everyone loved my boy.

Theo   Yes. He was kind.

Tries to return the money.

Aristo (*refusing the money*)   No, take it, you idiot, take it. But did everyone love *me*? Ah, that's the question. What do you think?

Theo   Everyone respects you, Mr Onassis.

Aristo   Oh, for Christ's sake, give me back the money.

Grabs the cash back from **Theo**'s *hand.*

Everyone hates me – you know that. They – in particular – *they* hate me.

Yanni   Who?

Aristo   They. Them. *Others*. Here, I don't want it.

Hands the money to **Yanni**.

They killed my Alexandro to get to me. Don't you
understand? It was an assassination by *proxy*.

To **Eleni**.

You loved him too, didn't you? From the time he was a
child. He was an attractive baby, wasn't he? I mean, taking
into account that babies are always ugly, he was a looker,
nonetheless.

Tugs the money from **Yanni**'s *hand*.

Give it to her.

Takes the money and gives it to **Eleni**.

Here. I want you to have this.

Eleni   No, Mr Onassis.

Aristo   Take it! I named him after my uncle, did you know
that? He was a passionate man, very political. The Turks
hung him in a public square. Turks! They are everywhere,
disguised, waiting ... Don't you believe me?

Aristo (*to audience*)   Pay attention!

To **Costa**.

Write these down. These are the possibilities. *Palestinians*.
Well, that's obvious, isn't it? They were sending me a
warning in code. My son's body was the code. Never, never
speak about Hamshari. That's what they were telling me.

Costa   Aristo ...

Aristo   If the world knew about Hamshari, they, the
Palestinians, would be totally compromised. They preferred
not to kill me, I might come in handy some day, some more
protection money maybe. So let's see, let's kill the son, that

will be our message to him. Kill the son. And Alexandro, of course, stupid boy, knew what had happened, thanks to his mother, his foolish mother, who told a child, a *child* – an innocent – things he must never hear. And they knew he knew. There are more listening devices in each of our houses than there are ice cubes. And that made him even more disposable.

Costa   Aristo, you are saying too much. Let's go back to the house.

Aristo   Excuse me? I give the orders, not you. Write. *Israelis.*

Another warning to me. If it were ever discovered that Bobby Kennedy's death was directly tied to the Palestinian leadership, well yes, Israel would win a few brownie points, but they would lose some as well – the American people might get fed up with the entire mess and wash their hands of it. The Israelis, of course, assume I'd blame Alexandro's death on the Palestinians. Just as the Palestinians would assume I'd blame the Israelis. *Or* it could have been Mossad and the Palestinian Secret Service working together. They have carried out joint operations, didn't you know that? Don't muck around with the Middle East. That's their message. And, of course, they're right. How could I have been stupid enough to walk into that cauldron? Has that disputed piece of geography ever led to anything but disaster? Connect them, please. Draw some lines. Right. Then there's the CIA. The FBI. The Mafia.

Their message? How dare you kill a Kennedy! That's what *we* do. Connect them.

And connect them to Israel and Palestine as well.

See how they criss-cross? They do each other's dirty work when it suits them. These days a bullet has many fathers. As do reversed cables. Connect them all! And throw in the oil companies – think how they must hate me, the ugly little Greek peddler, sailing his tankers into their rarefied

Protestant domain. And don't forget Greece itself. The Colonels are frightened of me. The Colonels are in bed with the oil barons and the oil barons with the CIA. Everyone's connected. Draw lines between all of them. They are all of them – Israel, Palestine, CIA, FBI, Mafia, oil, and yes, even Greece – all of them – Turks!

The names mentioned above come up on a screen, with connecting lines.

Aristo   OK, the picture is complete. The gods have had their little joke, haven't they? Perhaps they had their own plans for Bobby and I screwed them up. Who knows – perhaps they really wanted him to be elected president – and what? – bring justice to the land? Well, maybe he would have made the world a better place – fancy that. Odder things have happened. Whichever, I interfered with natural order, didn't I? It comes down finally to that, doesn't it? To me. The finger points directly to me. If I had simply given Hamshari protection money, nothing more, this would not have happened. My Alexandro would still be alive. My son would still be here – *annoying me* – annoying the hell out of me, the dumb prick, but *here* . . .

Weeps.

My son.

Eleni   No, no, it's not your fault . . .

Dimitra   You're just grieving . . .

Yanni   You're in shock . . .

Eleni   Don't blame yourself.

Aristo   Don't you dare give me sympathy. I do not accept condolences. I do not want pity.

Grabs the money from **Eleni**'s *hand.*

Give it back. That's mine.

Aristo *sits on the ground. He tears at his clothes. Then he walks to a tavern chair, and slumps into it.*

Eleni   He's making himself ill.

Dimitra   He's drinking too much.

Eleni   He's imagining things. Horrible things.

Theo   Do you really think Alexandro was murdered?

Dimitra   Who knows? *He* thinks so. That's all that counts.

Costa *drapes a shawl around* **Aristo***'s shoulders and walks him slowly downstage where he sits by the pool of water.*

Costa   His body is breaking down. He has a disorder of the autoimmune system. It usually hits men in their forties. He's proud of that, says it shows what great shape he's in. I think he's dying.

Jackie *enters.*

Jackie   Costa, I know.

Costa (*frightened*)   What do you mean?

Jackie   I know everything.

Costa   You do?

Jackie   How can I forgive him?

Costa   How did you discover ...?

Jackie   I overheard a telephone conversation. He's become careless. How could he do it?

Costa   I don't know. I'm ... I'm so sorry ...

Jackie   I mean ... drugs, of all things.

Costa   *Drugs...?*

Jackie   Yes. The Caribbean venture. I know all about it.

Costa (*starts to laugh*)   Drugs.

Jackie   Why is it funny?

Costa   It's not. I'm sorry. Nerves.

Jackie   He's running drugs. His tankers are transporting heroin from the Caribbean. Do you know how many young people that kills? How can you be a part of this, Costa?

Pause.

Costa   If you are attached to his life, you can afford a lot of soap.

Jackie   Has this been going on for a long time?

Costa   It's recent. Since he's been ill.

Jackie   Why?

Costa   Cash flow problems. He needed cash.

Jackie   What for?

Costa   A divorce.

Jackie   Oh.

Pause.

Jackie   I thought he was a pirate, not a gangster.

Costa   Can you be one and not the other?

Jackie   Probably not.

Jackie *starts to leave and then abruptly turns and walks into* **Aristo**'s *space. He is sitting on the ground, desolate. He doesn't see her. She stares at him and speaks, almost to herself.*

Jackie   Tick-tock … tick-tock …

Costa   What?

Jackie   Nothing.

Jackie *leaves.* **Yanni** *rushes in.*

Yanni   She's dead.

Costa   Who?

Yanni   His wife.

Costa   What?

Yanni His wife, permit me to say it, has died.

Costa His wife?

Yanni Mr Onassis' wife.

Costa Are you insane?

Yanni Bear in mind, they've been divorced many years.

Costa Oh. Tina.

Pause.

What happened?

Yanni I don't know. I was just told. She was found dead in Paris in the Niarchos apartment. Some say a heart attack, some say an overdose.

Eleni The mother of Aristo's children.

Yanni How much more can he take?

Eleni Where is he now?

Costa On the island, where he always is, at Alexandro's grave.

Aristo *sits by the grave. He brushes the soil surrounding it. The sea is heard in the distance.*

Aristo Now, your mother. Fourteen when I met her. I wasn't usually interested in 'green fruit' as we called it then. But she had golden hair and a tantalising smile and she already knew how to lie. And her father was the wealthiest ship-owner in the world. Do you smell the eucalyptus? You don't care about trees, do you? Well, tough shit, you're surrounded by them. Yes, she was a valuable prize, your mother. As was my second wife. Sometimes I hear melodies. In my head. There were musicians that played in a café in Smyrna near the harbour. Smyrna was the ancient home of demigods, did you know that? Mandolins, guitars . . .

The **Musicians** *start to play.* **Maria** *enters. She and the* **Chorus** *and* **Aristo** *all occupy separate areas.*

Maria   At the end of the day there is music. It's inescapable.

Aristo   There were almond trees – trees again, sorry, can't help it – jasmine, mimosa. No, my second wife was an even more valuable prize. There was nothing like her on the market. And at the time the price didn't seem like that much, really.

Maria   If I could sing to you, my dearest, I would. But, of course, now I can't. I suppose you saw to that.

Costa   What will happen to us when it's over?

Theo   Well, you, at least, will be able to bathe in it – for a long time after. There will be foundations to look after. And memoirs. I wouldn't worry.

Yanni   Bear in mind, some charities will benefit.

Dimitra (*to* **Costa**)   In time he'll become what you always wanted him to be – a hero.

Aristo (*to the grave*)   Forgive me.

Whispers.

Forgive me.

Maria   Well … you couldn't care less about Puccini anyhow, could you? You always wanted your own kind of music. Taverna music. Rebetiko.

Looks at the **Musicians**.

Aristo   The whores at Madame Fahria's were exquisite. They smelled of body powder. Coloured silk stockings. Fancy underwear. I was only fifteen, but I was learning. The fact that you had to pay for them only made them more desirable. You see, I fell in love – I fell *in love* – with women and transactions at the same time.

Pause.

I think eventually you'll grow to like eucalyptus.

Costa (*to audience*)   The doctors can do nothing for him. It's over. He just fades away.

Maria *walks down to the water.*

Maria   There's always a line on the horizon where the sea meets the sky. How many times did we stare at that? You taught me about the sea. When I was with you, it was as if time didn't exist. And now that's where we are – not exactly in the sea, not exactly in the sky. You mustn't be frightened, my darling.

Wades into the water.

I'm dead. We're all dead.

We're all memories now. Dust. Whatever. And soon a wind will come from the east – from Smyrna perhaps – and blow even that away. Do you know what I would like? I would like to see you dance one last time. Is that foolish? Or is it that I have to understand why I gave up so much? I don't know.

To **Others**.

Do you understand, my friends? *How could we love such a man?*

Pause.

I want you to dance. The way you would dance through my soul. Through my heart. The way you would dance for hours in the taverna, ignoring me, humiliating me. The way you would dance when you cheated on your mistress and your wife and your lovers as well and even the ladylike whores from Madame Claude's who were waiting in the wings. The way you would dance when you finessed a business deal that was so intricate and – well, Byzantine – that only a Greek – or, actually, a Turkish Greek – could ever understand it. The way you would dance when you were hungry – hungry for food, for love, for intrigue, for power, for pain, for deceit ... The way you would dance when you were alive ...

Aristo *rises and joins the* **Chorus**. *He walks down toward* **Maria**.

Maria   Damn you, Aristo. Damn you, my love. Dance.

She doesn't see **Aristo**, *but then feels his presence, and turns around.*

Aristo *dances.*